Bread and Olives

**Poems by
Fatima Hanan Elreda**

Copyright © 2018 Fatima H. Elreda
All rights reserved.
ISBN-13: 978-1720328162

Cover Design & Art Direction
Fatima Kassir

For Raúl and Zainab—
Your absence is a presence made
of stone
weighing heavily on my heart.

This land promises wheat and stars.
Worship it!
We are its salt and its water.
We are its wound, but a wound that fights.
—Mahmoud Darwish

CONTENTS

Acknowledgements
Introduction
Seasons of the Olive Tree 13

I. Winter

Fall 19
Mother Language 20
Taxi 21
Refugee Camp 22
Memory Room 25
The Harvest 26
Work of Art 27

II. Spring

Act of Resistance 31
The Road to Eternal Transience 32
Wheat Field 33
Home 34
Roots 35
Guts 36
Intifada 37

III. Summer

Breaking Bread	....	41
Drunk on Coffee	....	42
Let Us Write for Palestine	....	43
Requiem	....	44
Map	....	45
Where I Come from	....	47
Borders	....	50
The Color of Martyrdom	....	51

IV. Fall

Grateful	....	55
Bread	....	56
Dar	....	57
Walking through Ruins	....	60
How to Stitch up a Wound	....	61
To the Sun	....	62
The Olive Tree	....	64

ACKNOWLEDGEMENTS

This work would not have been possible without the support of Dr. Naheda Saad who paved the way for the creative project at the Lebanese University. I would also like to thank Dr. Adel Ismail for editing this edition and providing me with much-needed advice.

I am grateful to all of those who believed in me, to all of those who guided me when I needed guidance.

I wish to thank my family for always inspiring me. I am especially indebted to my husband who has been supportive in my pursuit of academic and creative goals. He is my backbone. I would like to thank my mother who is always there for me when I need her help and my son for making me want to be a better person in all aspects of life.

INTRODUCTION

Bread and Olives is a collection of poems on war, resistance, and identity in the Arab world. The opening poem "Seasons of the Olive Tree" traces the development of the olive tree as a symbol of resistance through the four seasons, each representing a phase in the fight for freedom. The book is divided into four chapters following the life cycle of the olive tree which begins with lethargy during winter when occupation plants death, agony, and displacement in the Arab land. However, this does not last long as spring gives life to the tree, and budding begins as a symbol of internal resistance and hope. As the tree grows through the summer, it begins to bear fruit while the struggle blossoms in the form of both physical and literary resistance to the Israeli occupation. The final chapter witnesses the harvest of the fruits borne by the olive tree which is indicative of the inevitability of victory when injustice is met with resistance. These poems speak of my relationship with the land and homeland but they also attempt to speak the common language of resistance that is transmitted through collective memory. Our grandparents tell us they lived on bread and olives, the staves of life that feed the love of the homeland. Thus, this book was titled ***Bread and Olives***, the bread made of the land's wheat and olives harvested from its trees.

Seasons of the Olive Tree

Winter

Green was the olive
that smeared our fingers with the scent of the South
and ripened our breaths.
Bitter was the aftertaste of the olive tree's bleeding fruit
crushed under the soldier's boot.
Silent were the leaves,
despite the crying winds.
Quiet were the thieves,
who lurked in the shadows.

Spring

By the fig and the olive, the book swears—
a blessed tree with a contorted trunk
extends its hands to the sky
and whispers a prayer.
Centuries and distances,
traveled the dove
from the ark of salvation
to the mountain of love,
till it reached a destination
and perched on a branch that did not bend,
but the journey has yet to end.

Seasons of the Olive Tree ────────────

Summer

A Gardener comes to pick the olives
but finds the blessed tree naked.
He cuts its throat, and then a flood
of blood
and tears—
as overflowing as their fears—
unearths the stumps that the roots once held.
They spoke to the sun
in branches of emerald.
Then, masked children
used their subtle hands to fill their pockets
with stones and bullets, evergreen;
some for their slingshots,
some for their older brothers—unseen—
to load their guns,
and some more for their fathers
to plant as seeds.

Fall

It
   was
      with
          the
             first
                falling leaf,

Bread and Olives

that the gems twinkled
and then were shaken,
beaten, wrinkled,
crushed, ground, and trodden.
But then the dove
took the fruit, bruised and sodden—
a message of hate and love.
And for that reason,
it was the harvest of the season.

Chequered was the veil,
that covered her face
when the horizon was swallowing the sun.
Thundering was the wail
when a handful of olives
were crushed in her bare hands.
From the golden oil
that oozed through her fingers
and drenched the soil,
she lit a lamp, kindled the fight
that inundated the land
with light.

Winter

Lethargy. Occupation. Death. Agony.

Fall

Words fall out of my head
like pieces of a broken mirror
or spilt water
on marble tiles.
A fallen leaf
reminds me of my grandfather's hand;
brownish yellow,
its veins burst out
and form mazes
that laugh at our fragility,
at our vulnerability,
and our despair.
It is death's final note
lying on the sidewalk.

Mother Language

The sea speaks in cursive
sending whispers to the shore
to say the unsayable
in a language that has braved time
but is drowning
slowly
in a vortex of abandonment.

Our language slips through our fingers
like sand sifting through time holes.
We fail to pronounce the words
emphatically
as the consonants die in our throats.

It floats before it sinks,
the letter that meets the sound—
as we read it from left to right.

Taxi

Sitting in the backseat of a taxi
on a rainy December day,
the driver turns on the radio,
a *Fairuz* song fills the car
with a tune of nostalgia
that both the old taxi driver and I feel.
An evil eye stone hangs from the cracked mirror
and swings
sketching invisible infinities in the air,
drawing blue waves.
There are droplets of rain on the window
and for once I'm not in a hurry.
I forget where I was going.
For once, I want to stay
inside a taxi:
a state of nowhere.

Refugee Camp

Smell

When you enter for the first time,
the stench of sewage invades you.
It strikes you violently—
not hard enough to knock you down
but just enough to make you light-headed
leaving an endless need to vomit
at the back of your throat.
You get used to the smell
as it infests your breath
but the nausea never subsides
and you wonder:
How do they breathe this air every day?

Sight

You can't unsee misery
once it hits your eyes.
It comes in different shapes and colors
many of which you can find in the camp:
in tangled electrical wires
and their shadows on the ground,
in **dark** alleys that seem to close on you
       and ones that lead you into a maze:
rusted iron doors
    laundry lines
        and graffiti walls
            culminate in visual ch^{a}o$_s$.

Sound

The sound of dampness
drips from the walls.
Yes, it is possible to hear stillness.
Silence does have a sound:
the faint ringing you think you hear when it's quiet
is really the noise made by water containers.
In the busy market,
vendors shout out,
and the noise of everyday is loud.
Beneath the hustle bustle
and the calls from the minaret
nostalgia hisses at you.

Touch

The first time I entered the refugee camp
I felt myself being pulled down
by the hands of the souls that lay beneath my feet.
My skin absorbed the sadness
that transmitted itself through the air
like a disease.

Taste

I cannot make out what it tasted like—
that feeling of being eternally dispossessed—
because how can I describe
the bitterness of homelessness
or the coldness of displacement?

Winter ───────────────────────

All I know it was acrid
and overwhelming.

The first time I visited a refugee camp
I learned that the senses there
are heightened and then numbed,
that some things meant to be momentary
can seem so permanent.

Memory Room

Take me to the memory room
and show me pictures, spoken memoirs,
the soul returning to the womb
as broken cries swing on the lips of fathers.

Take me to the memory room of my country,
of my people, of my nation
and show me the bent backs
lying in prostration.
Show me the blood stains on the white turban,
of the man leading rows of angels
and scattered pieces of flesh on prayer rugs.
Show me the broken shelves and the weeping Qurans.
Show me the clouds of black smoke billowing above a
silent minaret.

Lead me into the memory room
of now, and before, and to come.
Let me hear words of God bloom
on chapped lips and resonate through thirsty throats,
and let me breathe the blood-perfumed ether.
Let me see how the worshippers performed ablution
with their own red blood.
Tell me how they welcomed their absolution
with faint smiles on their faces.
It's true they broke their fast too early
for the time was not yet night,
and it may have been their last
but it was certainly not the least.

Winter

The Harvest

They called it *Grapes of Wrath*—
sixteen days of air raids
planting horror in the eyes of children,
rooting mothers' nightmares in the earth of their fears,
reaping souls that clustered under blankets of vine leaves.

Death came flying over the South in F-16s
to harvest lives before their time
to scatter the seeds of grief in the land
and watch them grow in the arms of fathers
that cradle the memory of their children.

In Qana,
the bitterest wine was shed;
the skin of children broke like bread.

Work of Art

War is a work of art
splattering buildings with bullets;
abstract, concrete,
meaningless, and incomprehensible to the inexperienced
eye.

It is a canvas that will forever be incomplete.

War is a work of art;
grotesque, surreal,
and hangs in a museum
against a wall of ideal.

We pay an exact price
to visit this place
to look at the portraits
and pretend to understand what they mean;
that is if they mean anything at all.

Secretly, we have no clue
what meaning this painting holds
or what it feels like to be within its folds.
But we gaze deeply into this work of art
because everyone else seems to admire it.

War is a work of art
a brush stroke of colors;
blood mixed with tears of mothers;
a distorted asymmetrical visage

of a million sisters and brothers.

War is a work of art
displayed in a gallery.
No one understands it,
but no one dares to admit it.

Spring

Budding. Memory. Hope. Inner *Intifada*.

Spring

Act of Resistance

Remembrance is an act of resistance
in a world that thrives on forgetfulness.
A rose that braves the cold
and blooms against the odds,
jasmine petals that remain white
in spite of the mud stains on our memory,
vines that climb old walls and conquer cement
speak the language of rebellion
reiterating:
"Remembrance is an act of resistance."

Spring

The Road to Eternal Transience

There's a road that takes you
not to heaven,
but to the closest thing there is
here
on this earth.

It's where the olive and the fig trees embrace.
It's the place you can't erase
from the folds of your memory.
It's where the scent of the soil,
rosewater, and olive oil
evaporate into your skin
and remain.

There's a road that leads you
not to forever,
but to a transient moment
that makes itself eternal.

Wheat Field

I run through a field of wheat
that begins on the side of the road
and ends at the edge of my memory.
It changes from green to golden
in a fraction of a second.
I don't know why,
but it feels like this place has been inside me
like I have been in it once before.
I can't put my finger on it;
there is no map that leads there
or a means to pinpoint it,
but I know it is there—
somewhere—
in the back of my mind.

Home

Home is not always a place.
For the lost, home does not have an address.

Sometimes it is a memory that you carry around
like the scent of your mother's scarf
or the fragrant basil leaves that grow near the window.

Small things that you can't forget:
the 99 beautiful names of God
(even if you can't recite them by heart),
or the smell of freshly baked bread
(even if you don't make the dough yourself),
or the smell of the earth on rainy mornings,
or gatherings at the table before breaking a day-long fast,
or hearing the call to dawn prayer,
(even if you don't wake up).

Sometimes you can take home with you:
a prayer rug, a book of poetry, a family portrait,
deeds to the lands of your ancestors,
keys with no doors to open.

But more often than not
home is just a memory
of what used to be,
and that can't be retrieved from an old box in the attic.

Roots

My roots are tangled
in the mess of yesterday,
and I can't seem to be able to separate myself
from the olive branch
that grows in my mother's womb,
the same way I can't pick the stars from the sky with my
bare hands
like figs.

My wound is too deep to heal on its own.
My pain is entrenched in the earth;
I can't dig myself up from the land of longing;
I am buried in a grave of yearning.
My roots are interwoven with memories I can't shake off—
not even the angriest storms can pull them out,
for they are embroidered in the fabric of my *abaya*:
my identity.

My roots run deep in the soil of history.
Like the wrinkles on my grandmother's face,
you can count the rings on the stump of the cypress tree
that grows in my memory
to determine how long I've been here.

Guts

When you question your own courage,
remember that David slew Goliath,
that Ahed slapped an Israeli soldier,
that she knows too much about tear gas and rubber bullets,
and that she is a child of the occupation.
Remember that she is not the only one
who was born into this generation,
growing up under a hovering cloud
of death and subjugation.

When you forget how to be brave,
remember that children in Gaza walk to school
under a sky that may rain rockets any day,
that their desks may be their only shield when that day comes,
that they draw portraits of absence,
and that they learn what fear is in the classroom
because they are never safe.

You only have to remember to muster the courage
and face your fear.
But it takes guts to make yourself remember.

Intifada

Rebel against your fears.
Throw rocks at your inhibitions.
Shout out at the silence.
Break the window of your passiveness.
Rise against injustice.

Spark an *intifada* in your soul.

Feed your anger the wheat of your land.
Release it from the grip of the branch
as if it were a ripe pomegranate
because bullets can't stop revolutions
that start within you.

Summer

Blossoming. Words. Stones. Resistance.

Summer

Breaking Bread

They want us to break bread
with those who steal our wheat,
burn our trees,
and claim we don't exist.
Don't they know
they're asking us
to share heaven with the devil
that has always sought to deprive us of it?
They want us to drink tea
with those who impose blockades
so that we don't have any.
They ask us to sit at a table
and talk about our fences over coffee
like old neighbours do.
Don't they know we are hospitable
only to those who enter our homes with no plans to evict us?

Drunk on Coffee

Arab poets get drunk on bitter black coffee,
cigarettes,
and *Fairuz*.
They write
with nothing to lose
but their own flesh.
In times of war,
they fight from their reading nooks
shielding themselves behind sandbags
that they replace with stacks of books.
"All up here!"
"And in here!"
A poet's hand quivers
as he points to his head and his heart:
"This is where the battle starts and this is where it ends."
Drunk Arab poets—
who gulp down shots of bitter black coffee—
crush the last of their cigarettes
in silver ashtrays,
believing the smoke in the room
is the smoulder rising from the site of an explosion
that has only occurred within them.

Let Us Write for Palestine

Let us write poetry for Palestine
on bullets, bread, and olives
and send them with love
in tightly-sealed bundles.

Let us write prose for Palestine
on laurels and vine leaves
with ink we make of cherry crimson.

Let us not throw away the seeds, either.
Let us enclose them in our letters to Palestine;
perhaps they could be sown;
perhaps they could be harvested in June.
Let us sing for Palestine
in a sweet melancholic tune
and pass the song to the nightingale
who will take our sorrows past the fenced trail.

Requiem

There is grief that awakens but never sleeps
like the tears that fill up your eyes
but never fall down your cheek.
They stick to your eyelashes
and drop inwardly
filling up your inner lake—
It is the soul that weeps.

From this grief,
you must compose a song.
Blow music into the *nay* that mimics the cries of the heartbroken,
that murmurs the lamentations of the exiled;
a requiem for the beloved
that could cross borders without visas
for the mourning homeless
who could send letters without a return address.

This grief is gusted into the flute at dawn
between the coarse fingers of a shepherd
whose face is a map of time
framed by a *kuffiyah*—
a requiem by the weeping *nay*
that is carried by the wind.

Bread and Olives

Map

On your map
there is a country called Lebanon,
and Beirut is its capital.
She is a lady
always reluctant to wear the dresses in her closet.
She is a woman
who would rather walk naked
than wear the attire of shame
or weave herself into a web of lies.
She is a woman hiding behind her veil
from the devouring eyes.
She is a woman whose body was raped
again and again,
but refuses to let her soul be raped as well.
On your map of geopolitics,
there is a country called Syria
sliced into pieces
partitioned into rations
for the ravenous nations.
Damascus in its heart,
its limbs are torn apart,
pulled from every side;
but she is still alive.
On your map of geopolitics
there is a small country
called "Israel"
raping lands, looting trees,
planting fear and anger,
reaping wheat, collecting defeat.

Summer

On your map,
there is a city
that changes her name
but never her identity,
for she knows history very well.
A thousand stories it could tell
about the people who pass by
and those who dwell.
On your geopolitical map,
there is a Jerusalem
but no al-Quds.
There is an Israel,
but there is no Palestine.
So we Arabs—
~~scratch that—~~
so every free soul
will burn your maps
and evade the semantic traps
you set.
We will call the land by its name.
We will not be the ones to blame.
We will draw our own maps
and follow the directions
that were imprinted on our skins
and weaved into our veins
with threads that meander through your checkpoints
to the city of prayer.

Where I Come from

Where I come from,
the smell of coffee
is infused with the scent
of sweet blood.
Where I come from,
the sound of prayer
is remixed with the cries of fathers
looking for their children
among the survivors,
lest they be dead.

Where I come from,
painters strike their brushes
on bridges that extend
from yesterday to tomorrow.
"Let's skip a day,"
they say,
"and paint red poppies
springing out of our wounds."

Where I come from,
death is a lie.
Where I come from,
angels do not dare fly
because their feet have been nailed to the ground
for so long,
for they walk among us
and their wings brush against our shoulders.

Summer

Where I come from,
men grab death from the arm
and draw it near.
Where I come from, men
embrace mortality.
Oh, if only I were a tear
suspending on their cheeks
between earth and heaven!

You ask me where I'm from.
I'll tell you where I'm from,
I am from the capital of dignity
and my country's name is freedom.
If you ask for my ID,
I'd show you pictures of a thousand martyrs,
you see,
they're the reason I'm here.

Where I come from,
the streets stink
of death,
of decomposing faith in humanity.
Where I come from,
they have silenced
the breath of sanity.

Bread and Olives

I am from a place that no longer exists on your map.
I am from nowhere;
I am from everywhere.
Wherever I'm from,
I'm there
and here.

Borders

They draw lines
to separate me from my land
as if it were possible for me to shed my skin
or dislocate myself from my own flesh.

Borders drawn on maps
demarcate nothing,
void as words spelled out in the air.
But when I hold the moon in my pocket
and wear wheat stalks in my hair,
I am in my homeland.

When my forehead absorbs the color of the sun
and the trees extend their shadows over my shoulders,
I am in my homeland.

When the minarets raise the call to prayer
and I answer that call,
my palms open wide and touch the earth;
I am in my homeland.

Lines on maps
don't demarcate my borders.
You can't besiege my identity
with barbed wire and cement walls;
it only knows the fragrance of my land.

The Color of Martyrdom

All the shades of green and blue and yellow
would not be without that crimson red
that all the martyrs gave the land
that all the martyrs bled.

All the wildflowers that eternally grow
on every mountain, valley, and riverbed
sprung out of the flesh and skin
that all the martyrs shed.

The martyr's blood falls, only to rise again—
As it waters the soil,
it gives life to land they thought was dead,
the one they now see covered
in that unmistakable red.

Fall

Harvest. Victory. Freedom. Resurrection.

Fall

Grateful

Sipping coffee on a September morning,
perched on a Beirut balcony;
she sees that the city has not awoken yet.
Still in her floral prayer dress,
reflecting the morning light,
she pours more of that black stuff
into the coffee cup.
She forgot to water her geraniums last night,
so she goes to fetch some water
for the white, orange, and red blooms.

In a white cotton shirt
and a rosary in one hand,
he recites some holy verses from
"The Exordium"
before he takes the cup and kisses it.
He is grateful for his being,
for the coffee cup,
for the woman in the prayer gown,
for September mornings on a balcony in Beirut,
and a sky clear of bombs.

Bread

We eat loaves of bread dipped in olive oil and thyme,
with a handful of olives and mint on the side,
and we are satiated
because we know that the bread
comes from the field of wheat that our fathers sow,
the one they water with the sweat of their foreheads,
because we know that our mothers grind, knead and bake it.
We are full because we know
that the olives come from our trees,
that our mothers preserve them in jars
to last the year in the cabinet;
because we know
that the thyme and mint come from the garden
that our grandmothers tend.
We eat loaves of bread soaked in olive oil,
and we are content
because the land gives them to us
and asks for nothing in return.

Bread and Olives

Dar دار

Home: دار

In the landscape of our existence,
we yearn for a place to call home;
rooms arranged around a center
like children swarming around their mother
under a star-lit ceiling.
It is called *Dar*.

But our language eludes us
setting traps for us to fall in,
swallowing our ignorance of its depth:
blending words and their meanings like olive oil and thyme
spreading the mixture on a piece of bread.

House: دار

We pack our luggage
or rather stuff it with the produce of our land
like grapevines,
as if it couldn't possibly be found anywhere else.

We insist that nothing tastes like home
or like the *moune*
stored in the cupboards of our
village house.

Homeland: دار

Still, we leave
because the land reeks of blood
and the walls are painted the color of fear,
because home stands on the edge of two abysses:
Death
and
Displacement.

Courtyard: دار

In the terrains of our nostalgia,
we build rooms around a courtyard;
and in our minds
we unlock doors,
water geranium pots,
and breathe in the jasmines
as if we have finally returned
from a long suffocating day at work.
That is where we take our afternoon tea.

Spun: دار

Among the meanings of this word
that twirls around us and itself
is the past tense of spin
(as in: *The memory of home spun around us until it was no longer a memory.*)
In a sense, all the meanings become one
once they blend with olive oil
and are applied over our blistering wounds.

Fall

Walking through Ruins

We move on
as we walk through the remnants of yesterday,
buildings reduced to rib cages.
Our lungs inhale the pregnant air
and exhale it pure.
We filter out the pain.

We move on
in infinite circles
on the wings of pigeons
that flock around minarets in unison.

We move on
as we pick up our things from the rubble,
and we take whatever pieces we can salvage
from ourselves.

We move on
making the ruins our homes,
fences of barbed wire,
beds from piles of rocks,
and windows from holes in the walls
carved by missiles.

We move on
exhuming the hope that was buried in the ruins
to rebuild ourselves;
we rise from the ashes.

How to Stitch up a Wound

When you are wounded,
you might bleed heavily,
so apply pressure to the cut;
a break in the continuity of being.
Remove foreign objects from the flesh:
cleanse it the way you would de-mine an orange grove;
close it the way you would lock the gate to your house;
let it heal the way you would mend a sparrow's broken wing.

To stitch up the wounds of a people,
you need to thread the needle first,
balance out the past and the present;
the sorrows and joys,
because one's presence is the absence of the other,
yet you cannot possibly separate them.

Puncture one end of the skin,
pull the thread of your existence
in spite of the throbbing pain.
Continue until the skin edges meet;
the place where closure begins
from the outside inwardly.

Embroider stories into the skin,
weave stars into the soon-to-be scar,
draw patterns that will remind you of how you got hurt,
seam the edges of the wound
that afflicts your soul.
That mark left on your skin
was inflicted by someone else,
but only you can stitch it up.

To the Sun

Expressing joy
in the midst of unrelenting grief
is the epitome of the human paradox;
the inexplicable absurdity of laughing uncontrollably
until you break out in tears.
Real tears
that have been kept inside for too long
find their way out
in a moment of fragility
amid a spate of laughter
like rain on a sunny day.

To the sun,
they hold out their palms
waving agonizing goodbyes
in the quietude of the morning
and they are somehow at peace
like a father
burying a martyred son
and laying a wreath of flowers
on his grave.

Beneath the sun,
they wait for their prisoners to return
from lost years,
knowing it will take time for them

to get adjusted to the light again.

To the sun,
they turn their gaze
as women in white scarves
pluck rose petals
and mix them with rice
so they would welcome those returning
from the darkness of imprisonment
into the light.

The Olive Tree

If the olive tree could weep,
it would shed oil instead of tears.

If the olive tree could mourn,
it would enshroud its grief
with silver leaves.

If the olive tree could fight,
it would carry itself through the grove
and throw olives instead of stones
at soldiers who threaten to uproot it from its home.

If the olive tree could speak,
it would weave its branches
into wreaths of victory.

GLOSSARY

Fairuz: an influential Lebanese singer whose songs are popular in the Arab world.

Abaya: a long garment or cloak worn by Muslim women, sometimes embroidered and decorated as part of local tradition.

Intifada: Arabic for uprising; often signifying the popular Palestinian uprisings against the Israeli occupation.

Nay: an Arabic form of the flute.

Kuffiyah: a chequered scarf traditionally worn by some Arab people.

Dar: Arabic for house, home, homeland, courtyard and the past tense of the verb spin.

Moune: provisions or food supplies.